MAGNETIC MARKETING

Learn Tired & Trusted Marketing Methods For Momentous Growth

Dr. Soobrata Dutta

INDIA • SINGAPORE • MALAYSIA

ISBN 979-8-88959-636-3

CONTENT

It feels like yesterday when I took Soobrata under my wing and started working together. I have coached and tutored hundreds of students throughout my career, and most of them went on to become impeccable icons in their respective fields. But Soobrata has always been exceptional. I still remember our first interaction; the strong positive vibes he gave out, and the burning passion he had for knowledge were enchanting. Right there, I knew that this boy would go on to do great things. As a life coach, I had seen and worked with so many extraordinarily gifted young men, but there was something different about Soobrata.

Soobrata and I met about 19 years ago, and since the day we met, we have been in a close mentor-mentee relationship. He is like a part of my family now! He did not come from a privileged background, nor was he one of those rich, private-school city boys. He came from a village unheard of, where he studied in a government school. However, the best thing is that his humble beginning never inhibited him from standing out and seeking the density he desired. He was never ashamed of his background and, indeed, never considered it a disadvantage. He came from a modest origin, but he always was proud of who he was, proud but never arrogant!

This book is one of Soobrata's dream projects. He has been working on this book for the last year and a half, and I am more relieved than him about its completion. Almost all my students are doing great in their lives, but none of them are writing books, as far as I know. Soobrata is the only one who went into writing after establishing a successful career. That should tell the reader a lot about his drive to achieve more and go further.

During the covid-19 lockdown, Soobrata came to me with the idea of this book, and he was quite passionate about it. It was going to be a manual for novice direct sellers, a map to help them navigate the tricky terrain of marketing. At the very onset, I thought it was a brilliant idea because most of the new network marketing professionals get caught in this marketing rut where they find no effective way to generate results or come out of it. When Soobrata explained the layout to me, I was pleasantly surprised by how meticulous he was and how he had everything planned beforehand. I received the book's first chapter by the end of the first week after this conversation. Soobrata called me up, and we had a two-hour-long discussion about it. It became a routine then; after finishing a chapter, he would call me, and we would discuss the entire thing.

So much research and effort have gone into this book. It is difficult for me to comprehend the level of dedication and commitment Soobrata has toward his readers. Even after working more than 12 hours a day, he always managed to give some time to complete this book. There are hundreds (if not thousands) of books about marketing, and most of them are quite well-written. They profoundly explore different marketing methods and strategies, but none of them address the fundamental marketing problems faced by new marketers and direct sellers. This book is devoted to that niche and audience, although I am certain intermediate and advanced professionals would also find this book helpful. This book will tell you everything you need to know to become an effective marketer and a network marketing professional. I believe these following pages have the potential to change your life if you are wise enough to implement them in your daily practices.

A strong drive and a learning attitude are all it takes to become the best! Keep these two things at your disposal; this book will give you phenomenal results.

-Dr. Debi Prasad Acharjya

INTRODUCTION
(CHAPTER 1)

Network marketing is a kind of selling that relies on people and uses their existing relationships to market a product or expand a business. These networks are used to find partners or clients and create leads. It is required of new recruits they go through a mentoring and training procedure.

Many new items were being developed during the 1880s industrial revolution with the intention of being sold to consumers. However, there was no explanation for the need for the products and no reason for the potential customers to purchase them, which is how networking marketing was introduced. After that, many big brands were established and this was how the network marketing industry started its journey.

If you want to start your business, then you should consider the following two things:

1.**Mentorship**: Mentorship is the secret to a successful life and a network marketing business.

2.**Learning, Research, and Market Study**: Researching your industry, doing a thorough market study, and learning network marketing can help you learn how to offer your products while keeping in mind the relationship you have with your customers.

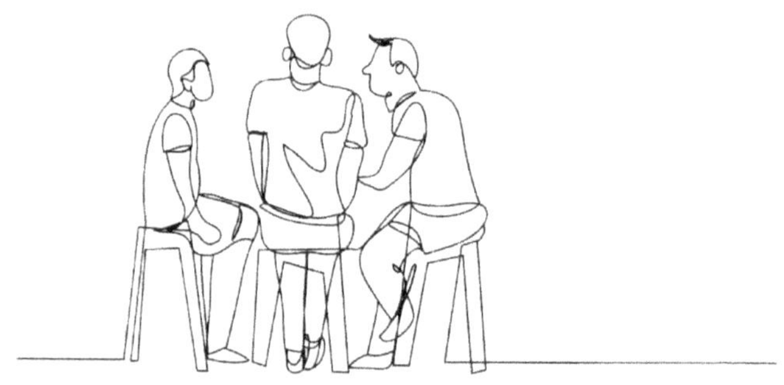

Marketing strategies are a collection of tactics you employ when approaching a consumer. This era is full of opportunities and interlinked with each other. One cannot prosper without the help of other.

Similarly, to grow your network marketing business you will have to implement the most successful marketing strategies.

That's because online marketing also known as digital markcting is a manageable and cost-effective route to reach more and more people while generating a good number of leads. This era is all about online platforms where people spend a lot of their time communicating with each other or finding answers to their doubts. In the coming chapters; I will give you a detail insight how you can use different platforms to drive more traffic and expand your network. But whether it is online or offline marketing, all the marketing strategies fall under one of two categories; it is either Pull or Push. Each category has its own significance and impact. The key to a good marketer is that he/she thoroughly comprehends both strategies and knows when to use each one.

Understanding the push and pull marketing strategies will enable you to determine the best method to use for your network marketing endeavours.

Growth does not happen naturally. If you want to expand your network marketing company, you must make decisions and act. You must comprehend the fundamental marketing methods if you want to increase your clientele, widen your network, and succeed as a network marketer or direct seller. Your tools of the trade are these marketing methods, which you should nurture and arm yourself with.

The push and pull marketing methods are the most fundamental ones. Once you master these techniques, you are on your way to becoming a successful direct seller!

In this book, we will go into detail about both push marketing and pull marketing strategies. We would explore their distinctions while also attempting to determine which one functions the best for your networking requirements.

I assume you are already a member of a reputable network marketing organization if you are reading this. After starting your direct selling career, you are now seeking methods to expand your network, develop your company, and steer yourself on the right path.

You might have a lot of questions like:

- How to approach your new customers?
- How to make your marketing investments more fruitful?
- What new strategies should you implement to gain better reach and response from the customer and sustain steady growth?
- What approach should you take to achieve your targets on time?

Network marketing, often known as direct selling, is a unique business concept. In this business model, you must be aware of how to establish trustworthy relationships with your customers. Only the conventional methods are not effective in network marketing. You need to know better and make smart decisions.

Therefore, to strengthen your strategy and prevent you from succumbing to a traditional mind-set, we have defined all the basics in this book. Continue reading to learn more.

WHAT IS PUSH MARKETING?

(CHAPTER 2)

The first marketing strategy we are going to explore is push marketing. Push marketing refers to a strategy, which a company uses to target a client directly with its goods, services, advertisements, and other types of material.

In push marketing, the business brings the product or service to the customers even when those customers aren't specifically seeking it.

Push marketing is sometimes referred to as outbound marketing and direct response marketing. When a company uses push marketing, its main goal is to use various media channels to generate market demand for its products or services.

They strive to instill a desire to buy the goods or services in their client's minds by exposing them to their products and services through promotions and advertisements. Push marketing's primary idea is to advertise your goods or services to your target market to create a desire for them to make a purchase from you. It is easy to understand.

Businesses that are fresh to the market frequently use push marketing techniques. They choose this direct strategy to secure their position in the market and reach the largest possible audience in a limited amount of time.

Push marketing is widely regarded as being excessively pushy and direct. Push marketing might help you achieve immediate results, but it is quite challenging to maintain the same results for a longer period.

- Let's understand push strategy through this diagram :

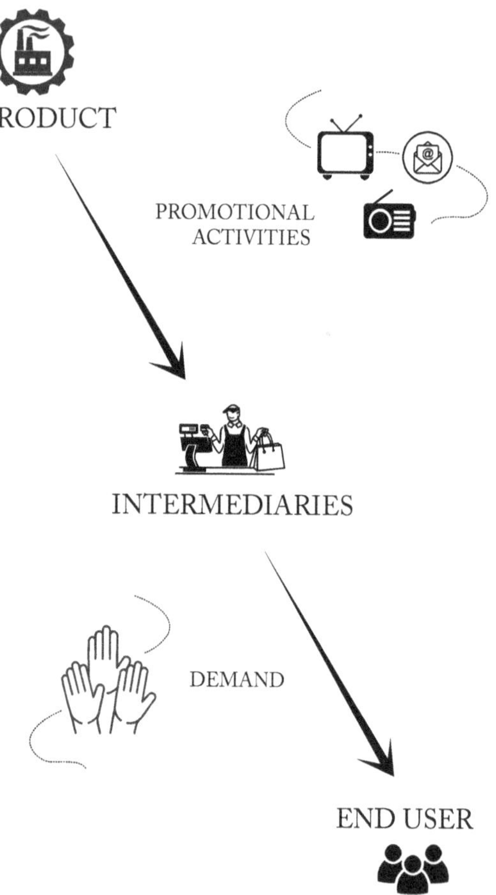

Implementation of Push Strategies:

Push marketing strategy has its way across various marketing channels. When companies use conventional advertising methods to convey their message to the customer. Here are some examples of Push Marketing to consider.

• Line Of Sight :

Line of sight is the procedure used when a new product is newly launched. For instance, a unique kind of energy bar. Retailers in the vicinity may be utilized to promote the new product by placing it on display at cash counters where customers can see it.

The location must be one where the target audience is already open to it. The presence of the product in a busy place encourages people to learn about it and propels them to buy it.

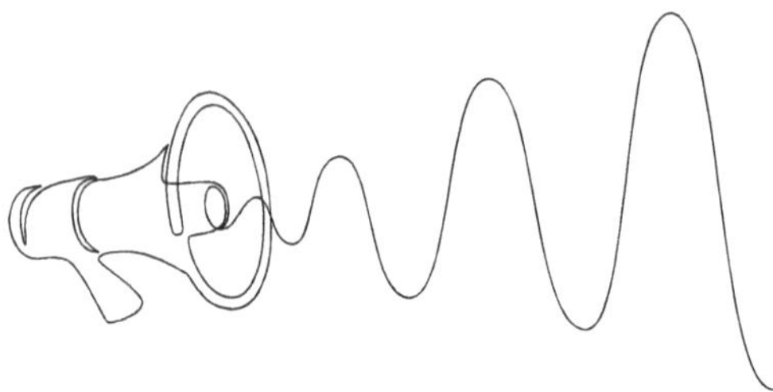

• TV Or Radio Ads :

TV and Radio commercials also fall under Push Marketing. If your company is about to launch a new product or service, then securing selected channels at specific times will help promote the products or services that will put the business up in front in the future.

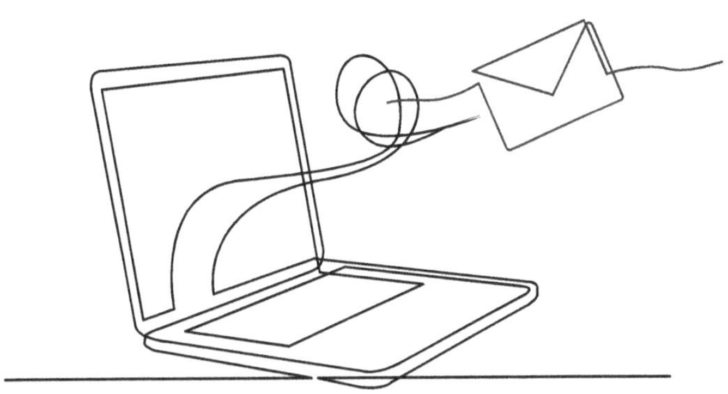

● Targeted Emailing :

Targeted emailing, cold emailing, and email marketing are also a part of the push marketing strategy. Here you send emails to your target demographic, highlighting your products and services. Email markcting helps you reach a more specific audience for your products and services. It also helps you expand your network and gain results faster.

● Outbound Marketing Strategy :

Outbound marketing strategy is an alternative name for push marketing that companies use for taking out their services or products to the customers.

Push Marketing – ADVANTAGES AND DISADVANTAGES:

■ ADVANTAGES

With the help of Push Marketing a company builds a wider audience reach. It helps in all ads that are created for both adults and kids.

It also raises awareness for your product, for example, you as a business owner want to promote your product, and you do that by creating a billboard on which you advertise your product or services. Therefore, more people come to know about it.

Push marketing offers you to get your customer with their feedback faster than pull marketing. You will get your customers in pull marketing as well, but the fastest and easiest way is always push marketing.

Push marketing is essential and useful for manufacturers who try to establish a sales channel along with seeking distributors to help with product promotion. With push marketing, your promotions will become easy and stable. Manufacturers always prefer this marketing over pull to start off.

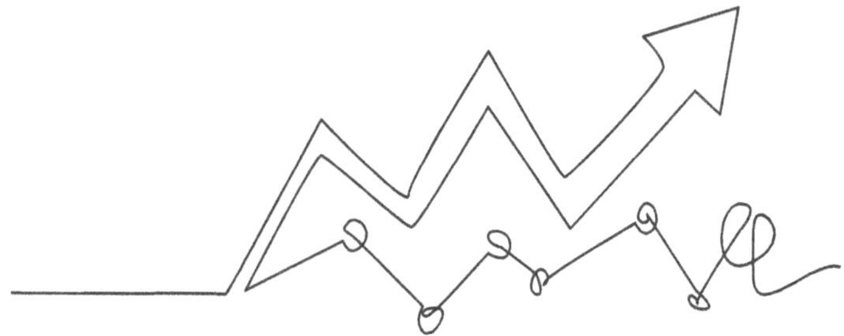

Not only that, but push marketing also creates product exposure, consumer awareness about a product, and product demand. Speaking of the demand, it can be more forecasting and predictable, as the producer has the capacity to produce and push as much or as little product to the consumers.

Economies of scale can help in realizing if the product is capable of getting produced at a scale due to high demand.

Push marketing also has disadvantages such as spending a lot of money for marketing purposes, if you decide to hold an event or launch ads.

If you display your ads everywhere, there can be issues of spam, and spam does nothing but make you lose your money and customers.

It requires an active sales team with the capability to work/network actively with retailers and distributors. The sales team is an integrated part of the company, the sale depends on their report.

Poor negotiating power with retailers and distributors can bring down the company therefore if the producers are the ones asking the retailers to stock their products, and the product may be a new one, therefore, not yet established as a profitable item for retailers to stock. This side of push marketing is harmful to the company or the person who summoned it.

For instance, if the product is new, it may be difficult to accurately forecast demand. And when one company fails to create demand for its products, the sale rate goes drastically down and ends up hampering the business.

Initial marketing efforts are known for being expensive. To answer why they are; it is more focused on securing a one-time purchase than on building customer relationships, trust, and loyalty. Therefore, the results may be short-lived.

Adverse consequences of the Push Strategy :

Push marketing aims to persuade resellers that they can make money off the items due to client demand or strong profit margins based on incentive reductions. Although a push approach frequently benefits suppliers, there are some potential short- and long-term downsides.

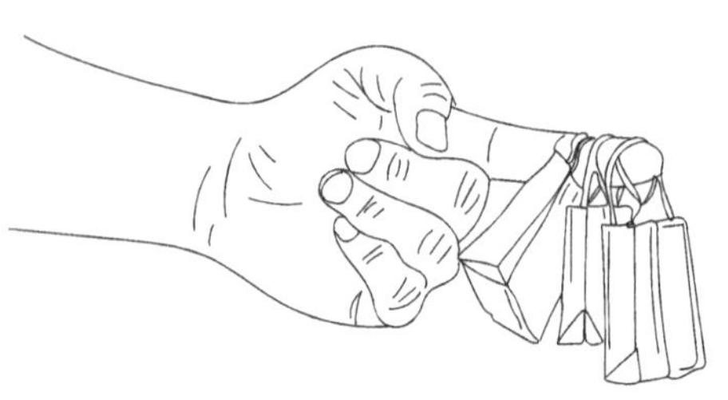

• Small Margins :

In push marketing, it's standard practice to provide resellers and clients discounts. Although this could encourage sales, it also implies that your enterprise is sacrificing part of its profitability by decreasing costs. Since businesses market each item cheaper than their actual production or procurement expenses, some businesses even suffer losses when providing concessions. This could aid in getting your goods onto store shelves and into the hands of consumers, but it takes a lot of time to make up for lost revenue.

● Reduced Provisions in the market :

The longer you use a push approach, the harder it is to convince distributors, sellers, and consumers to pay your standard rates because of the lower pricing approach. When you frequently give a discount, the resellers and consumers tend to become accustomed to them and perceive them as a necessary element of the deal, contrary to your hopes that the retailers would see such strong consumer demand that they will want to carry the goods irrespective of your pricing. Controlling the duration of time that discounts can help to prevent this. If they notice that you give discounts to rival businesses, other customers will anticipate them as well.

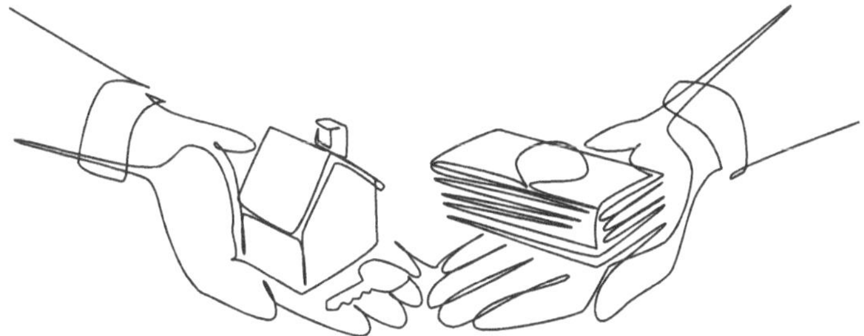

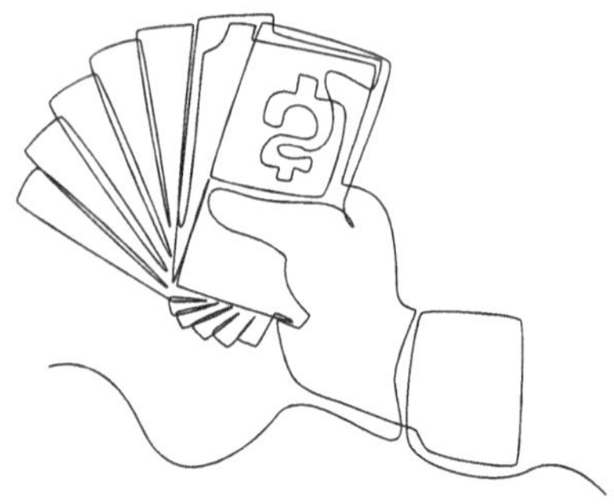

• Insufficient End-User Engagement :

Every cent and second spent on a push promotional campaign is time and money that might be spent on pull marketing, which involves building desire among customers. Given that their long-term performance depends on end customers; interests, vendors frequently attempt to strike a compromise between the two strategies. If you focus too much on advertising to your individual customers, you risk the consequences of not effectively conveying the advantages of your product to the consumer.

Push marketing is to introduce buyers to your brand, products, or services. Push marketing is to give a brand, product, or service the initial push it requires to establish itself in the market. This specific marketing is far more proactive and intentional compared to other inbound strategies.

Here are some instances that Push Marketing can do to help:

- Push marketing might be helpful when launching a company.
- It may be useful when introducing new items.
- Push marketing may be used to organize seasonal events.
- Push Marketing is used to support short-term initiatives and sales.
- Additionally, it is beneficial when switching to a different specialization.
- Push marketing is helpful when trying to increase revenue or sales.
- When the season ends, it aids in depleting the product supply.
- Push marketing assists in battling the market leader.
- It is regarded as the finest option for financing a multi-channel approach.

WHAT IS PULL MARKETING?
(CHAPTER 3)

The total opposite of push marketing is another type of marketing called pull marketing. Pull marketing focuses more on establishing demand so that clients actively seek out your products or services than push marketing, which primarily focuses on developing a desire for the things.

Pull marketing is a method used by established businesses to use existing reputation and brand image to create demand for their products and services. The pull approach also tries to meet market demand that already exists.

When you employ the push technique, you are pushing the products and services toward potential customers. However, when you employ the pull method, you want to attract clients to your business.

Pull marketing focuses on building a steady stream of returning consumers rather than generating quick, high-volume purchases. Instead of aggressively pursuing clients with your goods and services in this situation, you encourage them to locate your goods and services on their own.

Pull marketing is more effective than ever in the modern world. The internet and social media advancement has offered this technique countless new opportunities to the clients and accomplish your marketing objectives. The power of pull marketing techniques may be applied in various ways, from social media marketing to promotional strategy and discounts.

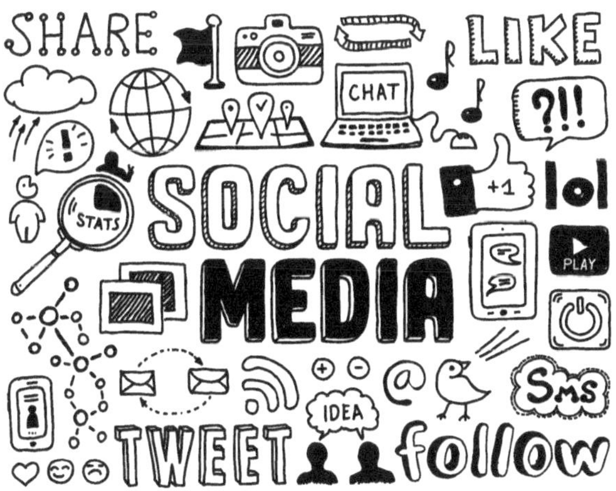

Pull marketing could be significantly beneficial because it doesn't only prioritize making sales. It also encourages proper growth and brand recognition.

- Client relationships
- Boost brand reputation
- Superior brand position

As was already established, pull marketing concentrates on building demand for a company's products and services so that customers would seek them out, which is the exact opposite of push marketing. Therefore, you can pull your customers to checkout and purchase your products and services by using:

• Social Media :

The densely populated domain of dormant clients is easily accessible in the realm of social media marketing. For instance, if you have the idea to launch a clothing line, Instagram advertisements will help you promote it more successfully than paying for advertising space in a newspaper or magazine.

The strategy aims to draw customers indirectly by making it appear as though they "accidentally stumble" into your advertisements.

Furthermore, it gives you access to millions of people throughout the world, making your target customers and selling regions much more diverse and lucrative.

• Cross Promotion :

Cross-promotion is an effective strategy for luring clients. A partnership with a website linked to your products and services is a terrific way to get visitors and increase sales.

For instance, if your company sells snow gear, collaborating with a website dedicated to winter activities will help you receive cross-promotional benefits and build brand recognition.

• SEO :

Everyone is aware of what SEO does. It is smart to use SEO to attract customers to your business because of its high ROI. You must implement all the effective SEO strategies and allow access to your website via keyword searches to attain a high yield from your SEO endeavours. When you implement practical SEO strategies, your products or services are likely to appear in front of people's eyes when they are seeking anything directly or indirectly related to your products or services.

Pull marketing is known as 'cost effective', the reason behind this is that the customers already know what they want. So, there is no need to build a huge advertisement to promote your services and products.

Pull marketing is better than push in terms of recognizing a customer's profile. There are various ways through which pull marketing can benefit your business.

For customers to gain quantitative insights, pull marketing creates a feedback mechanism and direct dialogue with customers. This method is good for your business if you have start-ups or have some new products to promote.

Pull marketing also helps in repeating business and strengthening customer loyalty.

This marketing boosts your brand and gives your product more value. Pull marketing helps reduce costs by cutting out excessive advertisement costs. It removes outbound marketing needs and attracts users to your services or products.

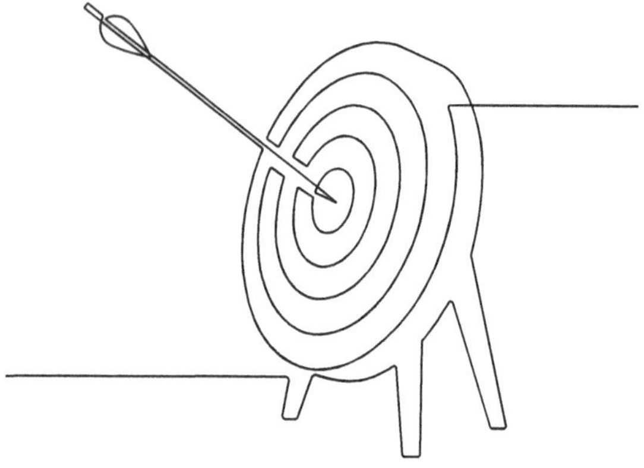

Just like advantages, there are disadvantages of this marketing such as you cannot reach as many customers as you want because you are already focused on the target market.

Other than that, pull marketing takes time to produce consistent outcomes or results. This strategy will not bring immediate consumers towards the product sales, as they are in their learning phase.

After knowing every detail about your product, the consumers will think of buying the product.

In a saturated market than other markets, pull marketing requires significant effort to create authority and product demand.

Pull marketing on the other hand entails exhaustive and intense research to build materials and use channels in order to make the targeted consumer grow desperate for your specific product

Here are some instances that Pull Marketing can do to help:

- Pull marketing can guarantee long-term commercial success for you and your organization.

- It aids in keeping control of a particular market or sector.

- It promotes loyalty and increases the number of repeat customers.

- Pull marketing aids in boosting brand awareness by increasing exposure and encouraging consumer interaction.

- It increases website traffic through referral, social segmentation, and organic means. It also encourages social media sharing.

- Pull marketing is regarded as the greatest when it comes to increasing sales since it generates income reasonably while reducing enormous advertising spending.

- Pull marketing also aids in connecting with clients while they are at the top of the purchasing funnel and are aware of their needs.

Pull marketing is just being aware of the eyeballs already interacting with the goods, knowledge, or services your business is already offering. Basically, pull marketing is leveraging that attention for your business goals. The company's sole responsibility is to employ pull marketing to direct customers to you in a straightforward manner.

Difference Between Push and Pull Marketing Strategies:

	PUSH	PULL
Strategy	Outbound	Inbound
Buying Journey	Brand Driven	Consumer Driven
Target	Mass Audience	Individuals
Channel	Mass Media	Search Engine
Constraint	Budget	Algorithms
Disciplines	Advertising, Direct Marketing, Public Relations	Content Marketing, Search Engine Optimization
Tactics	Advertising, Billboards, Mass Email, Press Releases	On-Page SEO, Blogging, Podcasts, Landing Pages

Charachteristies and the right time of usage :

	PUSH	PULL
Characteristics	• An effort in order to convince customers for making them buy a product. • It focuses on the Product's features.	• It is a passive strategy that holds attracting customers with desires and values • It focuses on aspirational values
Time of use	• Products valued by their features • For improved products • Technical products • For new products • For old products in new markets	• For simple products In strong brands • For common products • In well - known products • For mediocre products

The Most
Effective Marketing Strategy

(CHAPTER 4)

Now, we are fully equipped with the knowledge and understanding of the most distinguished marketing methods. We fully understand pull marketing and how it differs from push marketing tactics.

The topic of how to know pull marketing is the most result-yielding marketing tactic that has now emerged. Pull marketing is the most excellent method for various reasons, some of which are covered below.

The customer comes to you:

The first and most straightforward benefit of pull marketing is that the consumer comes to you rather than the other way around.

Why does it matter if the customer comes to us or if we go to the customer if the end result is still to make a sale, one will wonder?

That's where you're mistaken! The ultimate objective is to gain a loyal customer in addition to making a transaction. When you employ a pull marketing approach, you distinguish yourself from other brands by establishing yourself as a leader. It has been proven that when a consumer comes to you, it helps establish trust and credibility, which you can't establish through push marketing.

Long-term returns:

Sales and profits increase when you use a push marketing technique, but as soon as you stop using it, all the graphs start to fall. The pump-and-dump behavior of push marketing is unsuitable for the long-term growth of your sales and your business image. However, with the pull marketing strategy, that is not the case.

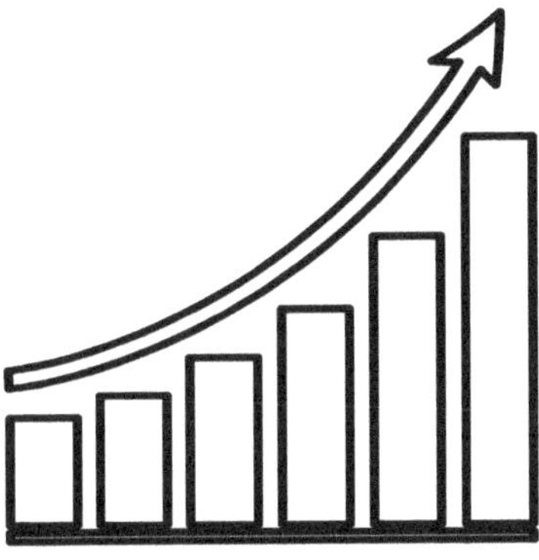

Utilizing a pull marketing approach will help you get consistent, long-lasting results. When you employ the pull technique, you don't only want to increase sales; you also want to establish a relationship of trust with your clients. As a result, having that mindset may help you attract devoted clients who stay with you for years and give your company a consistent cash flow over an extended period. Long-term returns and sustainable growth are always better than short and fast results.

Customer satisfaction:

Nobody can deny the significance of client satisfaction for a company's growth, development, and success in the market. One of the most critical factors in any organization is customer satisfaction, which affects all aspects of its growth and market image. The future of a business is determined by how satisfied its customers are with its products or services. Client satisfaction is also a measure of your quality. How pleased your customers are with your goods and services determines how the market views your brand.

Your development, credibility, and market reputation are all intimately correlated with customer happiness.

You might wonder how it relates to marketing strategies. The type of advertising used affects how potential customers feel about purchasing your goods or services.

The consumer always seeks to feel informed and intelligent. Push marketing can result in people buying products they don't need or desire, making them feel foolish later and making them hate your company.

Customers always choose your items when they independently locate them. They love your company because they think they are perpetually in charge. When it comes to marketing, the little things matter a lot. As a result, a marketer must always be attentive and meticulous.

Reach, Power, and Potential:

The reach, power, and potential of pull marketing have increased manifold with the advancement of technology. Thanks to the internet, pull marketing has an almost endless capacity to engage consumers, affect their decisions, and boost sales.

No objective would be out of reach for someone who employs internet marketing tools correctly.

Nowadays, it's rare to meet someone who does not own a phone or computer, making everyone a possible target for your marketing campaigns. If you know how to utilize it subtly, everyone's phone is like your own customized add screen.

Why does Push Marketing fail?

● **People don't like it:**

It cannot be more straightforward than that. Yes, it is common sense! Pushing a billboard, poster, or advertisement in someone's face is not the best way to win their loyalty or get them to purchase from you.

It could have worked a few decades ago, but not in the world, we live in now. Pushing advertisements into people's faces will only irritate them, which is terrible for your brand's reputation. Besides, the attention span of today's generation is concise, which works against push marketing strategies.

Push marketing accomplishes the opposite of what you want it to do: it makes people dislike you, discouraging them from showing interest in your goods and services.

● They see you as spam:

People begin to view you as spam when you continually use all marketing platforms to shove goods and services in their faces. People soon begin to avoid you. It is impossible to grow a business if people start disliking your image.

They ignore your calls, don't respond to your messages, and don't open the links you provide.

Because your persistent pressing makes you appear needy and desperate, they may occasionally even block you. It ultimately results in the loss of potential prospects and is detrimental to the marketer's morale.

● **It does not have any effect:**

Ultimately, the goal of any marketing plan is to make a good impression on people and use that impression to generate tangible results in the form of sales. However, push marketing falls short when it comes to fulfilling this fundamental objective.

When you compel somebody to do something they might not be interested in, it does not promote fruitful relationships or create favourable impressions. Instead, it establishes a barrier between the marketer and the audience, which results in unsuccessful marketing initiatives.

Therefore, it is always preferable to have a client come to you on his own rather than forcing your goods and services upon them. The latter entices people to leave. You should lure them in rather than shoo them away if you want more people to come to you.

Effects of Push Marketing:

Push marketing aims to generate short-term revenue. As I have discussed earlier it tries to push the customer toward the products or services. In order to that, push marketing creates a lot of consequences which ultimately cause long-term issues for the company.

Offers & Discounts Issues:

In push marketing, companies normally give offers, and discounts in order to make quick sales. Due to these offers, companies need to sacrifice a margin from their profitability. Moreover, consumer develops a habit of getting products cheaper than the MRP. So whenever companies try to withdraw the offers it will not be sold anymore. This could aid in getting your goods onto store shelves and into the hands of consumers, but it takes a lot of time to make up for lost revenue.

Hard to sell the product at the standard rate:

Starting from the distributors to end users as everybody tends to become accustomed to the discount and offers so it becomes very much harder to convince them to pay the standard rates. Now in such a situation, if the company tries to withdraw the offers, then two issues will be there:

i) The product will appear expensive to people and they will refuse to buy it

ii) They will start purchasing from another brand that is giving discounts on their products.

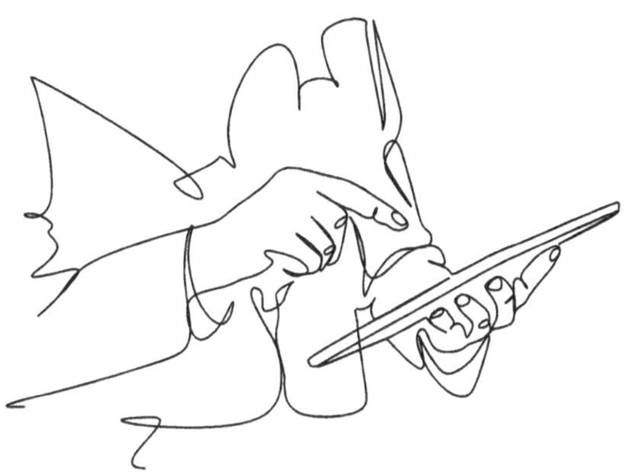

Too much expensive:

In push marketing, companies exhaust a huge budget in promotional activities in order to build the desire among the customer. Even after spending so much, no brand loyalty is developed in the customer's mind. They purchase it as they are getting good discounts on the products. In the future, if the discount is withdrawn the customer will not take this. So, the fact is it can not fulfill the long-term goal of any business.

How to Implement a Pull Strategy ?

Creating value for the consumer is the primary goal of a pull approach (not strictly monetary). It involves developing a reputation that draws clients to your goods even if you aren't explicitly promoting them. It involves creating a name that is synonymous with excellence, dependability, and trustworthiness.

It pertains to brand value. You must be aware that the marketplace (and your consumers) does not exclusively base their perception of the pricing of your items on quantitative considerations (such as quality of material and cost of production).

Your brand name determines the market worth of your goods. Your items will be seen as more precious and special if your brand has a better reputation in the market.

Pull marketing aids in building a solid reputation for your company in the marketplace as well as a brand name.

But how do you use pull marketing to associate value with your brand? How can you convince customers to prefer your products over those of your rivals? How can a pull strategy be implemented successfully?

In this section, we'll provide an answer to all these questions.

- **Create Good Content:**

You should start by producing quality content. But what constitutes quality content? The three primary characteristics of good content are that it has applicability in the real world, addresses relevant concerns, and solves problems. As long as your content is practical for the audience and adds value to their life, it will do magic for your brand image.

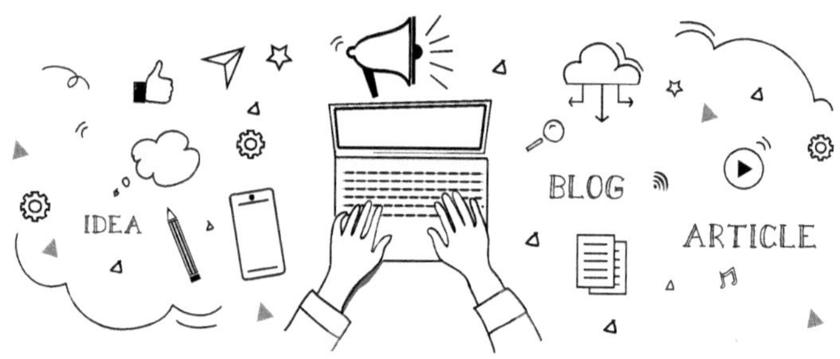

You must take your content game seriously and only publish relevant, relatable, and high-quality content. Every piece of content associated with your brand must be thoroughly examined before posting to ensure quality.

The primary aim of your content should be giving people what they need and resolving their problems because it is the best way to attract customers to your products and raise the brand's worth.

You can publish a blog or send newsletters addressing your industry's core issues. Doing this can win over clients' trust and pique their interest in learning more about your company.

• Communication is the key:

Knowing what your customers desire the best approach is to gain their loyalty and make your brand stand out as trustworthy and reliable.

However, you can offer them what they want only if you know what they want! Therefore, communicate with your customers.

You can accomplish it through a variety of tools, including email marketing and social media. There are countless tools available that let you speak with your clients directly.

You may learn more about your consumers' wants and needs by communicating with them. Additionally, it demonstrates your concern for your clients, which is essential to your long-term success.

• Use social media:

It is impossible to overestimate the impact that social media has on today's consumers. Social media significantly influences consumer behavior, decision-making, and brand development.

Social media is used by some companies to raise brand awareness, while others utilize it to increase website visitors and sales. Additionally, social media can help you build a community, increase brand engagement, and give your customers a way to contact you for customer service.

Go there and win the social media game if you want your customers to come to you.

• **Events and seminars:**

It is one of the traditional methods for developing your brand, even though it might seem obsolete and archaic.

Planning a seminar or traditional event is more beneficial to your professional development and business growth than you might think. It does not only help your business grow, but it also helps your management and interpersonal skills.

There are several benefits to planning various events and seminars, some of which include the following:

- They aid in spreading the word about your company.

- When someone sees you in person rather than on a screen, it is simpler to earn their trust.

- Displaying a posh location improves the perception of your brand.

- Building reputation and trust is a breeze with seminars and other activities.

Push Marketing - Pull Marketing or Both

(CHAPTER 5)

You can reap the benefits of your marketing endeavors only when you mix both pull and push marketing. Pull marketing and push marketing work well together. A push-and-pull marketing mix is necessary for your company to have a genuinely all-encompassing marketing plan.

Marketing is a creative art and innovative science. To have your voice heard, you must be inventive and decisive, but your strategy must also be focused and deliberate. You may create effective tactics for contacting your target audience by considering both your market and your clients. Push marketing and pull marketing are the two types of marketing that businesses utilize. Both have specific uses and shouldn't be used in combination. Here are some important facts regarding each.

A push marketing strategy may be the most effective if you are a new business with little awareness or an established business with a novel product offering. You may utilize pull marketing once consumers have recognized a need.

Push marketing is more advantageous for new businesses or when a person is introducing a new item or service. Raising awareness is essential since consumers would not be aware of your new product or services without push marketing.

Push marketing is also better suited for quick encounters than long-term relationship development.

You could draw customers to you and let them discover, consider, and determine what they require from you instead of trying to sell them something they may not be interested in. Each method has its advantages at specific periods, and both may be used in tandem to boost sales and client retention.

Today's consumers read testimonials and ratings, conduct their own inquiries, ask other people for recommendations, and utilize search to learn more about goods and services. Making your potential customers aware of your products or services should be your first focus as a marketer.

On the other hand, push marketing is more intrusive and compels the customer to respond immediately. You may therefore see faster revenues with push marketing.

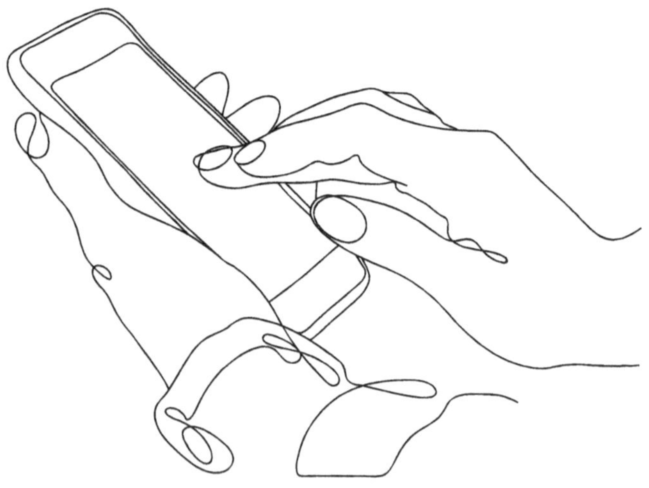

There are three crucial distinctions between the two marketing strategies:

• **Method**: Although pull marketing aims to increase awareness and establish brand identification, push marketing concentrates on increasing brand visibility and emphasizing distinctive selling propositions.

• **Stream:** Although it pulls promotional objectives from a much narrower audience through SEO, PPC, online marketing, etc., the push marketing strategy uses general media channels, including email, TV, radio, and in-person meetings.

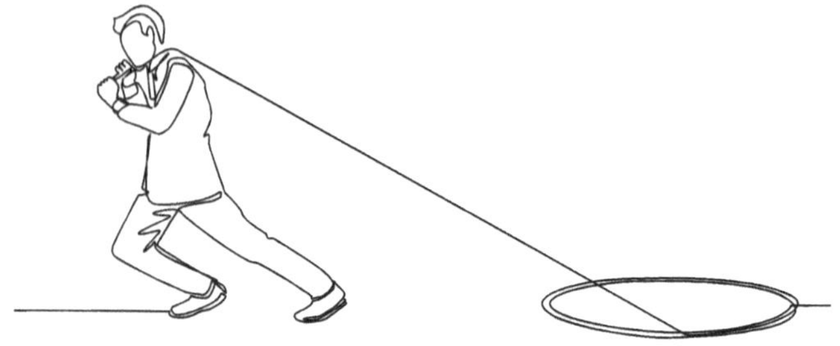

• Cost: Although pull marketing needs more effort on your part to interact consistently and communicate with consumers, push marketing is more expensive.

To establish the prospect funnel and generate demand for your products and services, you must learn and understand both methods. Pull marketing provides a means for customers to satiate that need once push marketing essentially creates the demand or desire.

1. Let us understand by some examples:

Not too long ago, when a beverage company partnered up with a Fintech company to give cashback to customers who bought a particular beverage brand.

Rational customers calculated the net price of the product after subtracting the amount received back as cashback.

They started buying cold drinks, but the retailers pushed them toward other cold drinks as they did not keep that beverage brand people were looking for. Although the substitute cold drinks do not carry the same reduced effective cost as the demanding one.

By this example, we come to know who played what part in the marketing game.

2. The beverage company created a PULL strategy and the retailers created a PUSH strategy.

Suppose you have gone to a mobile showroom in the hope to buy the one you want. But as soon as you tell the shopkeeper about your preference, he shows you but also tries to push you towards other companies. We all faced this push one way or the other while buying something.

Maybe the shopkeeper has their own agenda of getting a commission on the product he or she has been pushing you towards or just simply helping you to get out of the old beliefs. There is no doubt that the market is getting filled with improved and modified things every year. It is not a bad decision to try something new.

In this case, the mobile company that you wanted to buy from is doing PULL: attracting you to get your stuff from them.

The other two substitute mobile phone companies are being pushed to you.

How to Use Both Pull and Push Marketing Strategies

While implementing any marketing strategy there are various tips one can use to make sure of its success. Here are some tips to consider while using both pull and push marketing strategies.

• Make use of both online and offline marketing strategies.

• Make use of the available tools that help in determining how successful the marketing strategies are, and therefore make changes accordingly.

- Leverage any retailer connections if you have any while launching your products for additional exposure.

- If your brand is unknown, it is suggested to use a push strategy.

- Do a lot of research in finding your target audience, and make sure you are reaching them in the most effective manner.

Be a Consultant, Not a Salesman

In the selling industry the salesman does not only stay a salesman. There is a part called consultative selling, where a salesman must act as a consultant. The consultant helps in identifying the needs of the client such as external customers, your boss, and your team.

The job of being a consultant demands a higher level of credibility and trust than other sales models. If you are selling an idea to your executive board, your boss, or maybe the team and your current customers, you might want to focus on the relationship that is already there. If you find it, then use it as an advantage. Consultative selling not only helps you to do your sale but also your audience will find it as more intuitive and natural.

In this section, I will be giving you tips that have helped me become a good network marketer.

Be an expert in what you do

It is important for you to understand what is going on around you by analysing what your customers are going through every single day. You must understand what you are offering or what you are talking about and consult your clients on different topics even if it shows irrelevance compared to your products or services. So, keep doing research and do your homework by reading industry-related blogs or articles. Interact with your clients and build trust in the process.

Use your senses accordingly

The common mistake a salesperson makes is to think that a lot of talking about what their company has to offer is going to get a match. But the truth and fact are a salesperson must chalk out topics on which they are going to talk to their clients. Precise talking helps a lot.

Instead of talking too much about your company, its mission, vision, offers, products, and services, ask questions. Ask your client questions that would make them answer, give them logical reasoning, and then see how smoothly the meeting ends. During the process understand their problems and listen to them with absolute concentration. You cannot sell anything if you don't know what your client demands or requires.

Sell the problem, not the product

Understand that every client of yours has different needs and struggles; once you know tailor your tone accordingly. Make sure whatever you are selling is beneficial to your client and a solution to their problem. Ask them about their issues and know about the impact their problem has. Selling is not easy; you must give your best to convince them that their problem is somehow affecting their business and you have the solution that may change the situation.

Once you figure out how to penetrate his/her thoughts and plans, you will be known as a rational salesperson.

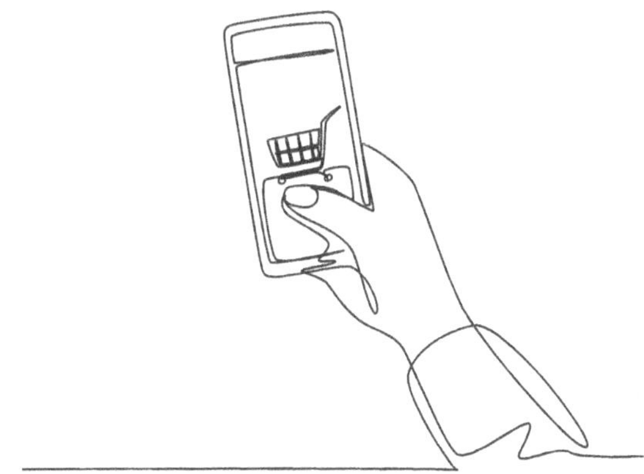

Relevancy matters

Always be polite while asking questions otherwise, it may look like you are arrogant or too much desperate to sell your product. The reason behind questioning someone should be the agenda of extracting all the information you need for your sales pitch.

It also lets everyone be a part of the conversation, otherwise, it would be boring to just sit and listen. Make your clients question you back, talk to them and bring up topics that interest them because that's how you can show them that your presence is needed and that you are there for them.

Do a background check?

It is important for you to know about your clients before you fix an appointment with your client. Not only about their company but also about them personally. No, I am not asking you to stalk them physically, but you can do it virtually, through LinkedIn or any other social media they have their presence on.

Research as much as you can, look for their company, and find out if they have launched any new product or held any press releases, or may have won any awards. If you talk to your client with all the information you have gathered, to them it will seem like you are genuinely interested to help them out.

Be confident in whatever you say, because the first impression creates an enormous impact on your client.

Push–Pull and Network Marketing
(CHAPTER 6)

Why is prospecting important in network marketing?

Prospecting is one of the most crucial components of network marketing success. It is the primary tool in your arsenal that you can use to grow, expand, and develop. In layperson's terms, prospecting means searching for potential team members who have the capability (if not skill) to take your network forward. It is a process of aggressively searching for and finding recruits.

Finding new team members, recruits, and customers are a significant issue for new direct sellers. As a new direct seller, prospecting seems like a major problem. However, it is not entirely their fault. They do have capabilities, but they need an excellent prospecting game. They connect with a lot of people but need help to convert!

I have broken prospecting into two major parts, one is finding people and the second part is converting or recruiting them. Most network marketers are good at the first part but fail when it comes to the second one.

Searching and finding people is easy. You can do it from the comfort of your home and even without leaving your bedroom with the help of the social media sites like Facebook, Instagram, LinkedIn, etc. But converting these prospects into customers or team members is the real challenge. And unfortunately, doing that part is not as simple.

I agree that finding people is a difficult task in itself. Sometimes the most significant barrier in prospecting is finding new people and having meaningful interaction with them. But with more than 18 years of experience in this field, I have learned some tired-and-trusted methods, which always helped me with both parts of prospecting. I will offer you valuable insights and advice gained over a period of 18 years of network marketing to help you overcome all the hurdles in prospecting and achieving your goals.

But before that, we shall discuss the two major types of prospects.

▪ Cold Prospecting

These potential recruits are completely unaware of your offerings, business, or services. At this stage of the prospecting process, your goal is to grab their interest in you and your offerings rather than trying to sell them a dream.

▪ Warm Prospecting

These potential prospects have expressed genuine interest in your business and services. All it takes is the appropriate advertisement and the opportune message to convert them and make them a part of your network.

Keep both these types of prospecting in mind because it is going to help us with our upcoming discussions.

Prospecting is crucial since it expands the possibilities. Consider it like this: converting a prospect to a team member takes time and might be challenging. However, it will generate a new income branch for your entire network, and The Compounding Effect gives you immeasurable benefits in the long run. Therefore, you must develop your prospecting game and learn to convert potential recruits without exhausting all your time and resources.

Furthermore, prospecting is vital because of its network expansion and personality development quality. Even when he is unable to convert a particular lead, he still gains valuable experience from the process. It also helps you from connecting with people outside your sector, which is essential for sustainable long-term growth. Prospecting is the driving force in network marketing and the most critical growth tool. One cannot think of prospecting and networking marketing as completely different entities. It is prospecting that makes network marketing possible!

Implementation of Push during prospecting :

Here is one of the most important questions: How and when do we implement push Marketing strategies while prospecting?

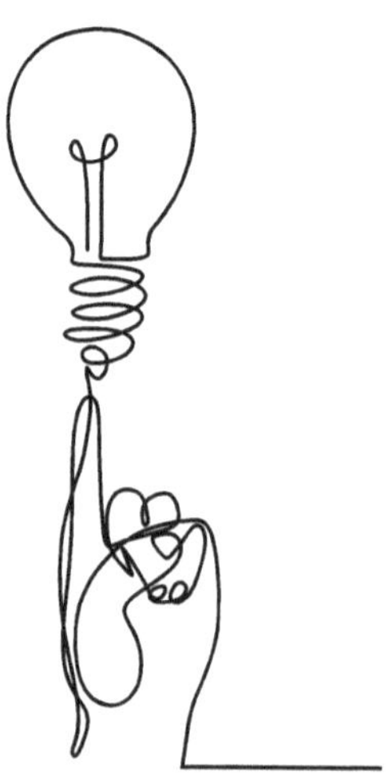

Remember, we already discussed Cold Prospecting. Cold Prospecting is when you make an offer to someone who knows nothing about your business, your profile, your services, and all the benefits that come with it. You need to start with push marketing when it comes to cold prospecting.

Benefits of using push for prospecting :

• Push Marketing helps you spread awareness and make your potential team members aware of all the benefits.

• It helps you overcome that initial inertia between the prospect and you.

• It helps you establish a communication platform and a proper prospecting channel.

• It helps you to increase your visibility and exposure.

Steps to implement push prospecting strategy:

1.Prepare, Prepare, and Prepare:

Preparation is the most important part of prospecting. You must be ready to answer all kinds of questions for the prospect's satisfaction. Therefore, know your playground and prepare everything; from your company's revenue in a specific year to the number of people joining each month. Think like a potential recruit and prepare with that mindset. If you are well prepared, you will be confident and confidence always sounds convincing to potential recruits.

2. Know Your Products : Before even thinking about prospecting, you need to know your products thoroughly. You need to make sure that you understand how the product relates to the market, how it will help people, how it will contribute to the growth of the company, and so on. Knowing your product and company thoroughly is essential to be a successful marketer.

3. Advertisement:

Push marketing is all about gaining exposure and making yourself seen, and to do that, you need to use every tool available to you. You need to systematically include all these tools in your prospecting strategy, from physical posters to social media. Think of anything that grabs your prospect's attention and use it. It could be discounts, gifts, seminars, etc. Use every advertisement tool to increase your exposure and get closer to your prospects.

Implementation of Pull while expanding your network :

Pull marketing is crucial for long-term success and expanding the network. You should use pull marketing when you are dealing with warm prospects. It helps you get better results and make the best use of your time and resources. While using pull marketing to expand your network, the fundamental principle to keep in mind is that you want to raise their interest so that they come to you, not the other way around.

Benefits of pull marketing:

- You have the upper hand in most interactions when you implement pull marketing.
- It helps you enhance your image and embellish the company's value.
- As the prospects are already showing interest, you do not need to work as hard to convert them.
- It gives you more reach as the people around your target also become interested in your products and company.

One of the most paramount things to understand is that the pull marketing strategy is based on producing content and advertisement that will attract prospects and then persuade them to join your network. To do this, material that addresses prospects' inquiries and concerns must be made available everywhere. Additionally, you must keep your ears open for all their questions and queries.

Here are some of the most effective pull marketing tools that will help you expand your network.

- **Social media marketing :**

To get the best results, you need the best methods. Social media marketing is one of the most powerful tools for pull marketing. It helps you directly target your prospects and feed them the content you want. Learn to use social media marketing in your pull prospecting and expansion strategy for the best results.

● Search engine optimization :

If you want to harness the internet's full potential, you need SEO. High-ranking search results can boost your visibility, which could bring more prospects to you and help you expand your network. Optimize all the content you put on the internet, and you will soon see more and more leads pouring in. But make sure that the content you put out maintains a high standard.

● Content :

As they say in digital marketing, "Content is the king." I believe it is true for every kind of marketing. If you deliver high-quality content to meet the interests and demands of your prospects, it becomes much easier to engage and convert them. To mirror the behavior of your potential prospects, your material should establish you as an authority in your field and specifically address the need you have discovered.

Why should you consider both?

Making your potential prospect aware of your presence should be your first goal as a network marketer. If your prospects don't know you exist in this market or don't realize what opportunity you are offering, all your marketing efforts are wasted, and you need to do better. Your need to enlighten the public necessitates the use of a push marketing approach. Inbound or pull marketing truly shines after people have recognized a need, and you need to make sure they discover you when they are looking for information. Therefore, separating one marketing method from the other is unintelligent, and using them both for their respective specialties is smart.

Push marketing establishes you as an authority in the market and gives you the necessary exploration and visibility. Pull marketing provides a means for people to satiate that need after first helping to create the demand or need.

Push and Pull marketing strategies have their benefits and drawbacks, so an integrated marketing strategy is essential to use the best of both worlds and foster long-term success.

Stepping into the world of network marketing is the most straightforward step towards a better career and the establishment of a huge network. However, there are so many more nurdles you must cross and many mountains you must conquer. The first one is recruiting more people and making yourself a recognizable brand, which can be done only with proper MARKETING.

When we talk about marketing, most of us think of advertising products and services, but marketing is so much more than that. It is an umbrella term that covers a lot more ground. It is about making yourself recognizable to larger masses, establishing trust in the market, and delivering products and services that consumers trust and cherish. Marketing is also about strategizing what to sell, how to sell, where to sell, what price to sell at, what characteristics to publicize, and so on. Promoting and advertising are small aspects of the whole marketing game.

It does not matter whether you are a beginner or a seasoned network marketing professional; we all need to fulfil some fundamentals in network marketing and follow them religiously. For instance, are you fulfilling the client's desires? Are you able to win your prospects' trust? Do the prospects have faith in you? All these questions reflect the fundamental requirement in network marketing: faith and trust.

What is the best way to accomplish these fundamentals?

Yes, you are right. It is marketing. Marketing is the answer to all these queries, and it is what helps you earn trust and win faith. Regardless of its form, marketing helps you engage your prospecting and help them realize that you are offering a once-in-a-lifetime opportunity. It also helps you expand your reach and create a sustainable demand in the market and beat your competition.

All-in-all, you can say that maintaining, growing, and expanding a lucrative network in today's world is impossible without marketing. Marketing plays a tremendous role in your success as a network marketer.

Learning and understanding marketing and realizing how it will benefit all the ventures of your life is a fruitful endeavour. And this book is your guide on the journey to understanding the relevance and application of marketing in the direct-selling field.

Your marketing approach has a vital impact on your success, and this book gives you the outline of a perfect marketing approach encompassing both push and pull marketing. It is a complete guide for beginners, intermediate marketers, and seasoned professionals. If you follow the layout of this book, you can grow your network, increase your revenue, and perfect promotional strategies, and accelerating your growth are a few examples of how the elements of this book will improve your life.

are a few examples of how the elements of this book will improve your life.

Your products and your company's name are never enough. You need more than that, and this is where you find it. The most crucial tool for any network marketer is awareness, and I have given you all the necessary components to develop that. Additionally, it boosts your confidence, enhances your reputation, and helps your sales.

As already discussed, push marketing is one of the best marketing strategies out there. Push marketing's objective is to encourage prospects to notice you and become aware of your offer. The central motivation behind this marketing strategy is exposure and expansion. Push marketing can be implemented through a variety of means, such as social media, regular mail, or physical posters.

Push marketing focuses on instant results and getting prospects ready for future presentations. Still, the smart network marketer always attempts to cultivate long-term relationships with his potential recruits alongside this technique. It's one of the most fantastic marketing tactics for boosting brand loyalty, gaining more exposure, laying the foundation of your brand, and increasing your product sales.

Push marketing is the most effective approach to getting results quickly and leaving a lasting impression on potential recruits. Yes, you may not be able to convert them instantly, but you will surely leave a mark on them. It fulfills all your branding requirements, establishes you as a trustworthy direct seller, and generates awareness about the products and services you have to offer. However, it can be a bit pricey, and the benefits are sometimes not as sustainable, but if you do it smartly, you can manage to convert more and more people even when you are putting in the least effort.

On the other hand, the goal of the pull marketing approach is to increase the number of potential recruits who desire to join your network. It is not as straightforward as push marketing, but it is as effective (if not more). It is about creating a marketing funnel that encourages people to contact you rather than the other way around.

Another approach to pull marketing is to form a marketing campaign that directly targets the prospects. A marketer must design the strategy in such a manner that it creates a desire in the prospects, and they themselves contact you for your offerings.

But pull marketing requires more time, and it works best when you have ample time to prepare effectively. When you put enough effort and time into the pull approach, the prospects come to you without feeling compelled to do so. Simply, pull marketing is when you persuade the customers to come to you without pushing your products, services, or benefits into their faces.

The most crucial element of pull marketing is authenticity and originality. It is difficult to make people come to you if you lack the quality and authenticity to persuade them. Furthermore, it is always recommended to use pull marketing when you are trying to establish yourself as a pioneer in any industry or field. When using pull marketing, your goal must always be to generate a lot of buzz, hype, and positivity for your business model. The more excitement you create, the better results you will get.

For many years, the advantages and disadvantages of push and pull marketing have been the subject of discussion. There is no end to this debate! However, the most experienced and knowledgeable marketing experts frequently include both tactics in their marketing efforts to deliver the best results. Whichever option you use, be sure to work with coordination, foresight, and give attention to detail.

www.ingramcontent.com/pod-product-compliance
Lightning Source LLC
Chambersburg PA
CBHW040141150726
48005CB00022B/1412